10 · 5 · 04

To Our Dear

On Your

Birthday

Love from
Jacqui & Simone

Youth is Wasted on the Young

Youth is Wasted on the Young

**Stephen Blake
and Andrew John**

First published in 2003 by
Michael O'Mara Books Limited
9 Lion Yard, Tremadoc Road,
London SW4 7NQ

ISBN: 1-84317-048-5

1 3 5 7 9 10 8 6 4 2
Cover image courtesy of The Norman Rockwell
Museum at Stockbridge. Printed by permission of the
Norman Rockwell Family Agency.
Copyright ©1933 the Norman Rockwell Family Entities

Designed and typeset by Design 23

Printed and bound in Finland by WS Bookwell, Juva

INTRODUCTION

Throughout history, people have always worried about getting older. About grey hair, physical decline and the ever closer threat of mortality. Today youth is an increasingly prized commodity, as the proliferation of anti-wrinkle creams, 'cures' for balding and plastic surgery indicates. Getting old, however, can still be something to celebrate, as such diverse figures as Bob Hope and Shakespeare have reflected. Maturity, wisdom and the benefits of experience can often – if not always – be age's rewards.

In this volume are gathered together quotes about youth and about age; about how age sees youth and about how youth sees age; about how age sees itself and both bemoans and celebrates the passing of youth. There are also the quotes stumbled across when looking for those about youth and age, such as those about the generation gap, about education and experience, about wisdom and ignorance.

Is youth really wasted on the young, as so many people have testified? Decide for yourself by tucking into this potpourri of quotations regarding society's preoccupation with youth and age.

A baby is an angel whose wings decrease
as his legs increase.
– *ANONYMOUS*

Middle age ... when a man is at the
peak of his yearning power.
– *WALL STRESS JOURNAL*

There must be a day or two in a man's life when he
is the precise age for something important.
– *FRANKLIN P. ADAMS*

Maturity is the ability to do a job whether or not
you are supervised, to carry money without
spending it and to bear an injustice without
wanting to get even.
– *ANN LANDERS*

In case you're worried about what's going to become of the younger generation, it's going to grow up and start worrying about the younger generation.
– *ROGER ALLEN*

There is absolutely nothing to be said in favour of growing old. There ought to be legislation against it.
– *PATRICK MOORE*

If children grew up according to early indications,
we should have nothing but geniuses.
– *Johann Wolfgang von Goethe*

Old age – when actions creak
louder than words.
– *Anonymous*

The best thing about getting old is that all those
things you couldn't have when you were young
you no longer want.
– *L.S. McCandless*

If you are truly serious about preparing your child
for the future, don't teach him to subtract – teach
him to deduct.
– *Fran Leibowitz*

Adolescence: a stage between infancy and adultery.
– *Anonymous*

The troubles of adolescence eventually all go away
– it's just like a really long, bad cold.
– *DAWN RUELAS*

Inside every adult lurks a graduation speaker
dying to get out, some world-weary pundit eager to
pontificate on life to young people who'd rather be
rollerblading.
– *KURT VONNEGUT*

I have found the best way to give advice to your
children is to find out what they want and then
advise them to do it.
– *HARRY S. TRUMAN*

At twenty years of age the will reigns; at thirty the
wit; at forty the judgment.
– *BENJAMIN FRANKLIN*

Age does not make us childish, as some say: it finds
us true children.
– *JOHANN WOLFGANG VON GOETHE*

That sign of old age, extolling the past at the
expense of the present.
— SYDNEY SMITH

Life should begin with age and its privileges and
accumulations, and end with youth and its capacity
to splendidly enjoy such advantages.
— MARK TWAIN

Youth has no age.
— PABLO PICASSO

Is that a birthday? 'tis, alas! too clear;
'Tis but the funeral of the former year.
— ALEXANDER POPE

All that I know I learned after I was thirty.
— GEORGES CLEMENCEAU

Old age is fifteen years older than I am.
– *OLIVER WENDELL HOLMES*

The young always have the same problem – how to
rebel and conform at the same time. They have now
solved this by defying their parents and copying
one another.
– *QUENTIN CRISP*

What America needs is more young people who
will carry to their jobs the same enthusiasm for
getting ahead that they display in traffic.
– *M.A. KELLY*

Middle age is when your age starts to show
around the middle.
– *BOB HOPE (attributed)*

Generation gap: A chasm, amorphously situated in time and space, that separates those who have grown up absurd from those who will, with luck, grow up absurd.
— *Bernard Rosenberg*

An archaeologist is the best husband any woman can have: the older she gets, the more interested he is in her.
— *Agatha Christie*

I am getting to an age when I can only enjoy the last sport left. It is called hunting for your spectacles.
— *Edward Grey*

You cannot put an old head on young shoulders.
— *Proverb*

As I grow older and older
And totter towards the tomb
I find that I care less and less
Who goes to bed with whom.
– DOROTHY L. SAYERS

Boys will be boys, and
so will a lot of middle-aged men.
– FRANK MCKINNEY HUBBARD

And the measure of our torment is the measure
of our youth.
– RUDYARD KIPLING

You are never too old to set another goal or to
dream a new dream.
– LES BROWN

First we are children to our parents, then parents to
our children, then parents to our parents, then
children to our children.
– MILTON GREENBLATT

Human beings are the only creatures on earth that allow their children to come back home.
— *Bill Cosby*

Human beings, who are almost unique in having the ability to learn from the experience of others, are also remarkable for their apparent disinclination to do so.
— *Douglas Adams*

The fact that boys are allowed to exist at all is evidence of a remarkable Christian forbearance among men.
— *Ambrose Bierce*

In America the young are always ready
to give to those who are older
than themselves the full benefits of
their inexperience.
— OSCAR WILDE

The lessons of the past are ignored and obliterated
in a contemporary antagonism known as the
generation gap.
— SPIRO T. AGNEW

The secret of eternal youth is arrested
development.
— ALICE ROOSEVELT LONGWORTH

There are so few who can grow old with a
good grace.
– SIR RICHARD STEELE

You've play'd and lov'd, and ate and drank,
your fill.
Walk sober off before a sprightlier age
Comes tittering on and shoves you from the stage.
– ALEXANDER POPE

Wisdom doesn't automatically come with old age.
Nothing does – except wrinkles. It's true, some
wines improve with age. But only if the grapes
were good in the first place.
– *ABIGAIL VAN BUREN*

Old fools are babes again.
– *WILLIAM SHAKESPEARE*

Old age equalizes – we are aware that what
is happening to us has happened to untold
numbers from the beginning of time. When we
are young we act as if we were the first
young people in the world.
– ERIC HOFFER

You've reached middle
age when all you
exercise is caution.
– ANONYMOUS

Don't worry about avoiding temptation – as you
grow older, it starts avoiding you.
– ANONYMOUS

Thou wilt fall backward when thou comest to age
For you and I are past our dancing days.
– WILLIAM SHAKESPEARE

The innocent and the beautiful
Have no enemy but time.
– W.B. Yeats

Enjoy the power and beauty of your youth. Oh,
never mind. You will not understand the power
and beauty of your youth until they've faded.
– Kurt Vonnegut

A boy becomes an adult three years before his
parents think he does, and about two years after *he*
thinks he does.
– Lewis B. Hershey

The longer I live the more beautiful life becomes.
– *Frank Lloyd Wright*

It has been said that there is no fool
like an old fool, except a young fool.
But the young fool has first to grow up
to be an old fool to realize what a damn fool
he was when he was a young fool.
– *Harold Macmillan,*
Earl of Stockton

Youth had been a habit of hers for so long that
she could not part with it.
– *Rudyard Kipling*

Before you contradict an old man, my fair friend,
you should endeavour to understand him.
– *George Santayana*

Wisdom before experience is only words; wisdom
after experience is of no avail.
– *Mark Van Doren*

What lies behind us and what lies before us are tiny
matters compared to what lies within us.
– *Ralph Waldo Emerson*

Find an aim in life before
you run out of ammunition.
– *Arnold H. Glasow*

One of the virtues of being very young is that you
don't let the facts get in the way of your imagination.
– *Sam Levenson*

Being young is greatly overestimated.
Any failure seems so total. Later on you realize
you can have another go.
– *Mary Quant*

When you are younger you get blamed for crimes you
never committed and when you're older you begin to
get credit for virtues you never possessed.
It evens itself out.
– *I.F. Stone*

The older I get, the better I was.
– *ANONYMOUS*

Do you know the difference between education and experience? Education is when you read the fine print; experience is what you get when you don't.
– *PETE SEEGER*

A truly great book should be read in youth, again in maturity and once more in old age, as a fine building should be seen by morning light, at noon and by moonlight.
– *ROBERTSON DAVIES*

Parents are the bones on which children sharpen their teeth.
– *PETER USTINOV*

When I was a boy of fourteen, my father was so
ignorant I could hardly stand to have the old
man around. But when I got to be twenty-one,
I was astonished by how much he'd learned
in seven years.
– *MARK TWAIN*

You will recognize, my boy, the first sign of old age:
it is when you go out into the streets of London and
realize for the first time how young the
policemen look.
– *SIR SEYMOUR HICKS*

**Deceive boys with toys,
but men with oaths.**
– *LYSANDER*

We see the brightness of a new page where
everything yet can happen.
– *RAINER MARIA RILKE*

It's not that age brings childhood back again,
Age merely shows what children we remain.
— *Johann Wolfgang von Goethe*

All would live long, but none would be old.
— *Benjamin Franklin*

Not by age but by capacity is wisdom acquired.
— *Titus Maccius Plautus*

When I grow up I want to be a little boy.
— *Joseph Heller*

By the time I'd grown up, I naturally supposed that
I'd be grown up.
— *Eva Babitz*

By the time we've made it, we've had it.
– *MALCOLM FORBES*

As long as you can still be disappointed,
you are still young.
– *SARAH CHURCHILL*

We should be careful to get out of an experience
only the wisdom that is in it – and stop there; lest
we be like the cat that sits down on a hot stove-lid.
She will never sit down on a hot stove-lid again –
and that is well; but also she will never sit down
on a cold one any more.
– *MARK TWAIN*

Experience is what causes a person to make new mistakes instead of old ones.
— *Anonymous*

Youth would be an ideal state if it came a little later in life.
— *Herbert Henry Asquith*

For certain people, after fifty, litigation takes the place of sex.
— *Gore Vidal*

Give me chastity and continence, but not yet.
— *St Aurelius Augustine*

> The first half of life consists
> of the capacity to enjoy without
> the chance; the last half consists of
> the chance without the capacity.
> — *MARK TWAIN*

Television has changed the American child from an
irresistible force to an immovable object.
— *LAURENCE J. PETER*

Children begin by loving their parents; as they
grow older they judge them; sometimes they
forgive them.
— *OSCAR WILDE*

Behold the child, by Nature's kindly law
Pleased with a rattle, tickled with a straw.
— *ALEXANDER POPE*

Children have never been very good at listening
to their elders, but they have never failed to
imitate them.
— *JAMES BALDWIN*

Having children makes one no more a parent than having a piano makes you a pianist.
– *MICHAEL LEVINE*

The best way to keep children home is to make the home atmosphere pleasant – and let the air out of the tyres.
– *DOROTHY PARKER*

Learning to dislike children at an early age saves a lot of expense and aggravation later in life.
– *ROBERT BYRNE*

It is no matter what you teach them [children] first, any more than what leg you shall put into your breeches first.
— *SAMUEL JOHNSON*

Old men are children for a second time.
— *ARISTOPHANES*

We write not only for children but also for their parents. They, too, are serious children.
— *ISAAC BASHEVIS SINGER*

Choose the life that is most useful, and habit will make it the most agreeable.
— *FRANCIS BACON*

Middle age is when you choose your cereal based upon the fibre, not the toy.
— *ANONYMOUS*

People who don't cherish their elderly have
forgotten whence they came and whither they go.
– *RAMSEY CLARK*

The misery of a child is interesting to a mother,
the misery of a young man is interesting to a
young woman, the misery of an old man is
interesting to nobody.
– *VICTOR HUGO*

Experience is a comb which nature gives us
when we are bald.
— *PROVERB*

Morality comes with the sad wisdom of age, when
the sense of curiosity has withered.
— *GRAHAM GREENE*

When it comes to age we're all in
the same boat, only some of us have been
aboard a little longer.
— *LEO PROBST*

Common sense is the collection of prejudices
acquired by age eighteen.
– *ALBERT EINSTEIN*

At sixteen I was stupid, confused and indecisive. At
twenty-five I was wise, self-confident,
prepossessing and assertive. At forty-five I am
stupid, confused, insecure and indecisive. Who
would have supposed that maturity is only a short
break in adolescence?
– *JULES FEIFFER*

How confusing the beams from memory's lamp are:
One day a bachelor, the next a grampa.
What is the secret of the trick?
How did I get so old so quick?
– *OGDEN NASH*

Consider well the proportion of things.
It is better to be a young June bug, than an
old bird of paradise.
– *MARK TWAIN*

Towering in the confidence of twenty-one.
– *SAMUEL JOHNSON (quoted by Boswell)*

What I look forward to is continued immaturity
followed by death.
– *DAVE BARRY*

The surest way to corrupt a youth is to instruct him
to hold in higher esteem those who think alike than
those who think differently.
– *FRIEDRICH NIETZSCHE*

**If youth but knew;
if age but could.**
– *HENRI ESTIENNE*

It takes courage to grow up and turn out to be
who you really are.
— *E.E. CUMMINGS*

You cannot create experience. You must undergo it.
— *ALBERT CAMUS*

The atrocious crime of being a young man …
I shall neither attempt to palliate nor deny.
— *WILLIAM PITT, EARL OF CHATHAM*

Old age is … a lot of crossed-off names
in an address book.
— *RONALD BLYTHE*

There is still no cure for the common birthday.
— *JOHN GLENN*

The old complaint that mass culture is designed for eleven-year-olds is of course a shameful canard. The key age has traditionally been more like fourteen.
– ROBERT CHRISTGAU

How beautiful is death, when earn'd by virtue!
Who would not be that youth? What pity is it
That we can die but once to serve our country!
– JOSEPH ADDISON

> You can't turn back the clock.
> But you can wind it up again.
> — BONNIE PRUDDEN

We must always change, renew, rejuvenate
ourselves; otherwise, we harden.
— JOHANN WOLFGANG VON GOETHE

Old men are dangerous; it doesn't matter to them
what is going to happen to the world.
— GEORGE BERNARD SHAW

I have been dead for two years,
but I don't choose to have it known.
— LORD CHESTERFIELD

It costs a great deal to be reasonable. It costs youth.
— MADAME DE LA FAYETTE

Life is pleasant. Death is peaceful.
It's the transition that's troublesome.
— ISAAC ASIMOV

The fundamental defect of fathers, in our competitive society, is that they want their children to be a credit to them.
— *Bertrand Russell*

The denunciation of the young is a necessary part of the hygiene of older people, and greatly assists the circulation of the blood.
— *Logan Pearsall Smith*

Describing seventy as the golden age is a modern form of alchemy.
— *Elliott Priest*

Women deserve to have more than twelve years
between the ages of twenty-eight and forty.
– *JAMES THURBER*

Age does not diminish the extreme
disappointment of having a scoop of
ice cream fall from the cone.
– *JIM FIEBIG*

Years ago we discovered the exact point, the dead
centre of middle age. It occurs when you are too
young to take up golf and too old to rush to the net.
– *FRANKLIN P. ADAMS*

The first sign of maturity is the discovery that the volume knob also turns to the left.
— *JERRY M. WRIGHT*

At fourteen you don't need sickness or death for tragedy.
— *JESSAMYN WEST*

Don't mess too much with your hair or by the time you're forty it will look eighty-five.
— *KURT VONNEGUT*

We can draw lessons from the past, but we cannot live in it.
— *LYNDON B. JOHNSON*

Each man carries within him the soul of a poet who died young.
— *SAINTE-BEUVE*

From the earliest times the old have rubbed it into
the young that they are wiser than they, and before
the young had discovered what nonsense this was
they were old too, and it profited them to carry on
the imposture.
– *W. SOMERSET MAUGHAM*

My idea of education is to unsettle the minds of the
young and inflame their intellects.
– *ROBERT MAYNARD HUTCHINS*

We've put more effort into helping folks reach old age than into helping them enjoy it.
– *FRANK A. CLARK*

I'm not forty, I'm eighteen with twenty-two years' experience.
– *ANONYMOUS*

I am old enough to see how little I have done in so much time, and how much I have to do in so little.
– *SHEILA KAYE-SMITH*

I have everything now that I had twenty years ago, except now it's all lower.
— *GYPSY ROSE LEE*

Everything has been said before, but since nobody listens we have to keep going back and beginning all over again.
— *ANDRÉ GIDE*

The old believe everything, the middle-aged suspect everything, the young know everything.
— *OSCAR WILDE*

The foundation of every state is the education of its youth.
— *DIOGENES LAERTIUS*

Youth, which is forgiven everything, forgives itself nothing: age, which forgives itself anything, is forgiven nothing.
— *GEORGE BERNARD SHAW*

What do we ever get nowadays from reading to equal the excitement and the revelation in those first fourteen years?
– GRAHAM GREENE

As for me, except for an occasional heart attack, I feel as young as I ever did.
– ROBERT BENCHLEY

If we could sell our experiences
for what they cost us,
we'd all be millionaires.
– ABIGAIL VAN BUREN

The clamour
Of childish days is upon me, my manhood is cast
Down in the flood of remembrance, I weep like a child for the past.
– D.H. LAWRENCE

What is youth except a man or a woman
before it is ready or fit to be seen?
– *EVELYN WAUGH*

We pay when old for the excesses of youth.
– *J.B. PRIESTLEY*

The spiritual eyesight improves as the physical
eyesight declines.
– *PLATO*

It is a youthful failing to be unable to
control one's impulses.
– *Seneca*

The Child is father of the Man;
And I could wish my days to be
Bound each to each by natural piety.
– *William Wordsworth*

Fair in the cradle and foul in the saddle.
– *Proverb*

I am resolved to grow fat, and look young till forty!
– JOHN DRYDEN

'You are old, Father William,' the young man said,
'And your hair has become very white;
And yet you incessantly stand on your head –
Do you think, at your age, it is right?'

'In my youth,' Father William replied to his son,
'I feared it might injure the brain;
But, now that I'm perfectly sure I have done,
Why, I do it again and again.'
– LEWIS CARROLL

I don't feel old. I don't feel
anything till noon. That's
when it's time for my nap.
– BOB HOPE

To find a young fellow that is neither a wit in
his own eye, nor a fool in the eye of the world,
is a very hard task.
– WILLIAM CONGREVE

Few people know how to be old.
— *FRANÇOIS, DUC DE LA ROCHEFOUCAULD*

A child is not a vase to be filled, but a fire to be lit.
— *FRANÇOIS RABELAIS*

Filth and old age, I'm sure you will agree,
Are powerful wardens upon chastity.
— *GEOFFREY CHAUCER*

In the depth of winter, I finally learned that within
me there lay an invincible summer.
— *ALBERT CAMUS*

Young men are fitter to invent than to judge, fitter
for execution than for counsel, and fitter for new
projects than for settled business.
— *FRANCIS BACON*

**When you are about thirty-five years old,
something terrible always happens to music.**
— *STEVE RACE*

You know, when I first went into the movies Lionel Barrymore played my grandfather. Later he played my father and finally he played my husband. If he had lived I'm sure I would have played his mother. That's the way it is in Hollywood. The men get younger and the women get older.

– *LILLIAN GISH*

At my age flowers scare me.

– *GEORGE BURNS*

Yes, time flies. And where did it leave you? Old too soon … smart too late.

– *MIKE TYSON*

Children are the only form of immortality that we can be sure of.

– *PETER USTINOV*

It's all that the young can do for the old, to shock them and keep them up to date.

– *GEORGE BERNARD SHAW*

Old people are fond of giving good advice:
it consoles them for no longer being capable of
setting a bad example.
– *FRANÇOIS, DUC DE LA ROCHEFOUCAULD*

Old age is not for sissies.
– *BETTE DAVIS*

Men at forty
Learn to close softly
The doors to rooms they will not be
Coming back to.
– *DONALD JUSTICE*

Forty is the old age of youth; fifty the
youth of old age.
– *VICTOR HUGO*

The lovely thing about being forty is that you can
appreciate twenty-five-year-old men more.
– *COLLEEN MCCULLOUGH*

Whenever a man's friends begin to compliment
him about looking young, he may be sure they
think he is growing old.
– *WASHINGTON IRVING*

From forty to fifty a man must move upward, or
the natural falling off in the vigour of life will carry
him rapidly downward.
– *OLIVER WENDELL HOLMES*

Youth is a disease from which we all recover.
– *DOROTHY FULHEIM*

The older generation thought
nothing of getting up at five
every morning – and
the younger generation
doesn't think much of it either.
– *JOHN J. WELSH*

We receive three educations, one from our parents, one from our schoolmasters, and one from the world. The third contradicts all that the first two teach us.
– CHARLES LOUIS DE SECONDAT, BARON DE MONTESQUIEU

We learn from experience that men never learn anything from experience.
– GEORGE BERNARD SHAW

I never think of the future – it comes soon enough.
– ALBERT EINSTEIN

Put your future in good hands – your own.
– *ANONYMOUS*

Men are wise in proportion not to their experience
but to their capacity for experience.
– *JAMES BOSWELL*

Do not go gentle into that good night,
Old age should burn and rage at close of day;
Rage, rage, against the dying of the light.
– *DYLAN THOMAS*

People who get nostalgic about childhood were
obviously never children.
– *BILL WATTERSON*

They say genes skip generations. Maybe that's why
grandparents find their grandchildren so likable.
– *JOAN MCINTOSH*

The great thing about getting older is that you don't
lose all the other ages you've been.
– *MADELEINE L'ENGLE*

We know we're getting old when the only thing we
want for our birthday is not to be reminded of it.
– *Anonymous*

In gallant trim the gilded vessel goes:
Youth on the prow, and Pleasure at the helm.
– *Thomas Gray*

They love the Good; they worship Truth; they laugh
uproariously in youth;
(And when they get to feeling old,
They up and shoot themselves, I'm told).
– *Rupert Brooke*

It is good for a man that he bear the
yoke in his youth.
– *Lamentations*

Old age, believe me, is a good and pleasant thing. It is true you are gently shouldered off the stage, but then you are given such a comfortable front stall as spectator.
– *Jane Harrison*

Good judgment comes from experience, and experience – well, that comes from poor judgment.
– *Cousin Woodman*

Life is a moderately good play with a badly written third act.
– *Truman Capote*

There's many a good tune played on an old fiddle.
– *Samuel Butler*

Whom the gods love dies young.
– *Menander*

Grandchildren don't make a man feel old: it's the knowledge that he's married to a grandmother.
– *G. Norman Collie*

The reason grandparents and grandchildren get along so well is that they have a common enemy.
— *SAM LEVENSON*

Nobody grows old merely by living a number of years. We grow old by deserting our ideals. Years may wrinkle the skin, but to give up enthusiasm wrinkles the soul.
— *SAMUEL ULLMAN*

As we grow older we grow both more foolish and wiser at the same time.
— *FRANÇOIS, DUC DE LA ROCHEFOUCAULD*

I don't plan to grow old gracefully. I plan to have face-lifts until my ears meet.
— *RITA RUDNER*

Do not regret growing older.
It is a privilege denied to many.
— *ANONYMOUS*

Growing old – it's not nice,
but it's interesting.
– *AUGUST STRINDBERG*

Growing old is no more than
a bad habit which a busy
person has no time to form.
– *ANDRÉ MAUROIS*

It's difficult to decide whether growing pains are
something teenagers have – or are.
– *ANONYMOUS*

You will find as the children grow up that as a rule
children are a bitter disappointment – their greatest
object being to do precisely what their parents do
not wish and have anxiously tried to prevent.
– *QUEEN VICTORIA*

Age is no guarantee of maturity.
– *LAWANA BLACKWELL*

You can't help getting older,
but you don't have to get old.
– *George Burns*

For the first half of your life, people tell you what
you should do; for the second half, they tell you
what you should have done.
– *Richard Needham*

A child's hand in yours – what tenderness it
arouses, what power it conjures. You are instantly
the very touchstone of wisdom and strength.
– *Marjorie Holmes*

If I were young and handsome as I was, instead of old and faded as I am, and you could lay the empire of the world at my feet, you should never share the heart and hand that once belonged to John, Duke of Marlborough.
– *SARAH, DUCHESS OF MARLBOROUGH (refusing an offer of marriage from the Duke of Somerset)*

Happiness in old age is, more than anything else, preserving the privileges of privacy.
– *HAROLD AZINE*

Life would be infinitely happier if we could only be born at the age of eighty and gradually approach eighteen.
– *MARK TWAIN*

Children aren't happy without something to ignore, And that's what parents were created for.
– *OGDEN NASH*

The ageing process has you firmly in its grasp if you never get the urge to throw a snowball.
– *DOUG LARSON*

The teenager seems to have replaced the Communist as the appropriate target for public controversy and foreboding.
— *EDGAR FRIEDENBERG*

The young have aspirations that never come to pass, the old have reminiscences of what never happened.
— *SAKI (HECTOR HUGH MUNRO)*

By the time I have money to burn, my fire will have burnt out.
— *ANONYMOUS*

Young men have a passion for regarding
their elders as senile.
– *HENRY BROOKS ADAMS*

Young people have an almost biological destiny
to be hopeful.
– *MARSHALL GANZ*

I think age is a very high price to pay for maturity.
– *TOM STOPPARD*

It is hard to convince a high school student that he
will encounter a lot of problems more difficult than
those of algebra and geometry.
– *EDGAR W. HOWE*

My father didn't tell me how to live: he lived, and let
me watch him do it.
– *CLARENCE BUDINTON KELLAND*

I don't know how you feel about old age … but in my
case I didn't even see it coming. It hit me from the rear.
– *PHYLLIS DILLER*

Young men wish: love, money, and health. One day,
they'll say: health, money, and love.
– *PAUL GÉRALDY*

I am ashes where once I was fire.
– *LORD BYRON*

I like the dreams of the future better than the
history of the past.
– *THOMAS JEFFERSON*

I'm not interested in age. People who tell me their
age are silly. You're as old as you feel.
– *ELIZABETH ARDEN*

Idealism is what precedes experience;
cynicism is what follows.
– *DAVID T. WOLF*

When I was a boy the Dead Sea was only sick.
– *GEORGE BURNS*

> If age imparted wisdom,
> there wouldn't be any old fools.
> — CLAUDIA YOUNG

The most important thing that parents can teach
their children is how to get along without them.
— FRANK A. CLARK

In a dream you are never eighty.
— ANNE SEXTON

We grow grey in our spirit long before
we grow grey in our hair.
— CHARLES LAMB

In youth we run into difficulties; in old age difficulties run into us.
– *JOSH BILLINGS*

Old age is an incurable disease.
– *SENECA*

Insanity is hereditary: you can get it
from your children.
– *SAM LEVINSON*

Information's pretty thin stuff unless
mixed with experience.
– *CLARENCE DAY*

Fun is like life insurance: the
older you get, the more it costs.
– *FRANK MCKINNEY HUBBARD*

Intelligence, in diapers, is invisible.
And when it matures, out the window it flies.
We have to pounce on it earlier.
– *STANISLAW J. LEC*

Age is not an accomplishment,
and youth is not a sin.
– *ROBERT HEINLEN*

Beauty is but a flower
Which wrinkles will devour …
– *THOMAS NASHE*

Advanced old age is when you sit in a
rocking chair and can't get it going.
– *ANONYMOUS*

The trouble with ageing is that, by the time you finally know your way around, you don't feel like going.
– *ANONYMOUS*

The answer to old age is to keep one's mind busy and to go on with one's life as if it were interminable. I always admired Chekhov for building a new house when he was dying of tuberculosis.
– *LEON EDEL*

It well becomes a man who is no longer young to forget that he ever was.
— *SEIGNEUR DE SAINT-ÉVREMOND*

It's hard for me to get used to these changing times. I can remember when the air was clean and sex was dirty.
— *GEORGE BURNS*

There is nothing wrong with today's teenager that twenty years won't cure.
— *ANONYMOUS*

Give one boy a job to do, and you get half a job done; give two boys a job to do and you get no work at all.
— *ANONYMOUS*

It's not that I'm afraid to die, I just don't want to be there when it happens.
— *WOODY ALLEN*

Age is just a number.
– *ELISE WILLIAMS*

Just at the age 'twixt boy and youth,
When thought is speech, and speech is truth.
– *SIR WALTER SCOTT*

Keep true to the dreams of thy youth.
– *FRIEDRICH VON SCHILLER*

When you are young you take the kindness
people show you as your right.
– *W. SOMERSET MAUGHAM*

One of the delights known to age, and beyond the grasp of youth, is that of Not Going.
– *J.B. PRIESTLEY*

Knowledge comes, but wisdom lingers.
– *ALFRED, LORD TENNYSON*

If a little knowledge is dangerous, where is the man who has so much as to be out of danger?
– THOMAS HENRY HUXLEY

Of course there's a lot of knowledge in universities: the freshmen bring a little in; the seniors don't take much away, so knowledge sort of accumulates.
– A. LAWRENCE LOWELL

You know you're getting old when all the names in your black book have MD after them.
– ARNOLD PALMER

Childhood is Last Chance Gulch for happiness. After that, you know too much.
– TOM STOPPARD

A lady of a 'certain age', which means Certainly aged.
– LORD BYRON

You're only as young as the last time
you changed your mind.
– TIMOTHY LEARY

The idea is to die young as late as possible.
– ASHLEY MONTAGU

You don't stop laughing because you grow old. You
grow old because you stop laughing.
– MICHAEL PRITCHARD

Learn all you can from the
mistakes of others.
You won't have time to
make them all yourself.
– ALFRED SHEINWOLD

Anyone who stops learning is old, whether at
twenty or eighty.
– HENRY FORD

Whoso neglects learning in his youth,
Loses the past and is dead for the future.
— *EURIPIDES*

I'm very pleased to be here. Let's face it, at my age
I'm very pleased to be anywhere.
— *GEORGE BURNS*

Never let the future disturb you. You will meet it, if
you have to, with the same weapons of reason
which today arm you against the present.
— *MARCUS AURELIUS ANTONINUS*

Age is opportunity no less than youth itself.
– *Henry Wadsworth Longfellow*

The farther behind I leave the past, the closer I am
to forging my own character.
– *Isabelle Eberhardt*

Men fight for liberty and win it with hard knocks.
Their children, brought up easy, let it slip away
again, poor fools. And their grandchildren are
once more slaves.
– *D.H. Lawrence*

You can tell a child is growing up when he stops asking where he came from and starts refusing to tell where he is going.
– *ANONYMOUS*

Life consists not in holding good cards but in playing those you hold well.
– *JOSH BILLINGS*

Life is a long lesson in humility.
– *JAMES M. BARRIE*

Old age is life's way of punishing us for having the audacity to have been young.
– *BARNABY JOHN*

The older one grows, the more one likes indecency.
–*VIRGINIA WOOLF*

There's no fool like an old fool.
— *ANONYMOUS*

Don't limit a child to your own learning, for he was born in another time.
— *RABBINICAL SAYING*

Rushing design is like rushing growing up. You suffer mightily sooner or later or both.
— *WWW.BEFORETHEARCHITECT.COM*

Literature is mostly about having sex and not much about having children. Life is the other way round.
— *DAVID LODGE*

The first forty years of life give us the text; the next thirty supply the commentary.
— *ARTHUR SCHOPENHAUER*

If I had my life to live again, I'd make the same mistakes – only sooner.
— *TALLULAH BANKHEAD*

When I can look Life in the eyes,
Grown calm and very coldly wise,
Life will have given me the Truth,
And taken in exchange – my youth.
– SARA TEASDALE

Who well lives, long lives; for this age of ours
Should not be numbered by years, days and hours.
– GUILLAUME DE SALLUST, SEIGNEUR DU BARTAS

An old man looks permanent, as if he had
been born an old man.
– H.E. BATES

Old age realizes the dreams of youth. Look at Dean
Swift; in his youth he built an asylum for the
insane; in his old age he was himself an inmate.
– SØREN KIERKEGAARD

When you have loved as she has loved, you
grow old beautifully.
– W. SOMERSET MAUGHAM

It's funny how most people love the dead, once you're dead you're made for life.
– *JIMI HENDRIX*

Therefore my age is as a lusty winter,
Frosty but kindly.
– *WILLIAM SHAKESPEARE*

A young man is embarrassed to question
an older one.
– *HOMER*

When you're a young man, Macbeth is a character
part. When you're older, it's a straight part.
– *SIR LAURENCE OLIVIER*

Every man over forty is a scoundrel.
– GEORGE BERNARD SHAW

The imagination of man's heart is evil
from his youth.
– GENESIS

Make wisdom your provision for
the journey from youth to old age,
for it is a more certain
support than all other possessions.
– BIAS OF PRIENE

'Beware of the man who works hard to learn
something, learns it, and finds himself no wiser
than before,' Bokonon tells us.
– KURT VONNEGUT

Middle age is when you've met so many people
that every new person you meet reminds you of
someone else.
– OGDEN NASH

Youth is a malady of which one becomes cured a little every day.
– *BENITO MUSSOLINI*

An old man loved is winter with flowers.
– *GERMAN PROVERB*

By the time a man notices that he is no longer young, his youth has long since left him.
– *FRANÇOIS MAURIAC*

The follies which a man regrets most in his life are those which he didn't commit when he had the opportunity.
– *HELEN ROWLAND*

The four stages of man are infancy, childhood, adolescence and obsolescence.
– *ART LINKLETTER*

To know how to grow old is the masterwork of
wisdom, and one of the most difficult chapters in
the great art of living.
— HENRI FRÉDÉRIC AMIEL

In love, as in other matters, the young
are just beginners.
— ISAAC BASHEVIS SINGER

I have my whole life to be mature, why start now?
— ANONYMOUS

A man not old, but mellow, like good wine.
— STEPHEN PHILLIPS

Age to me means nothing. I can't get old: I'm working. I was old when I was twenty-one and out of work. As long as you're working, you stay young. When I'm in front of an audience, all that love and vitality sweeps over me and I forget my age.
– GEORGE BURNS

Men are but children of a larger growth.
– JOHN DRYDEN

To be mature means to face, and not evade, every fresh crisis that comes.
– FRITZ KUNKEL

Age is an issue of mind over matter. If you don't mind, it doesn't matter.
– MARK TWAIN

Middle age is when a narrow waist and a broad mind begin to change places.
— *ANONYMOUS*

In a man's middle years there is scarcely a part of the body he would hesitate to turn over to the proper authorities.
— *E.B. WHITE*

The dead might as well try to speak to the living as the old to the young.
— *WILLA SILBERT CATHER*

Old age puts more wrinkles in our minds than on our faces.
— *MICHEL EYQUEM DE MONTAIGNE*

One of the pleasures of middle age is to find out that one *was* right, and that one was much righter than one knew at say seventeen or twenty-three.
— *EZRA POUND*

It's a mere moment in a man's life between an all-star game and an old-timers' game.
— VIN SCULLY

Live as long as you may, the first twenty years are the longest half of your life.
— ROBERT SOUTHEY

The longer I live the more I see that I am never wrong about anything, and that all the pains that I have so humbly taken to verify my notions have only wasted my time.
— GEORGE BERNARD SHAW

The older I grow the more I distrust the familiar
doctrine that age brings wisdom.
– *H.L. MENCKEN*

Most people think life sucks, and then you die. Not
me. I beg to differ. I think life sucks, then you get
cancer, then your dog dies, your wife leaves you,
the cancer goes into remission, you get a new dog,
you get remarried, you owe ten million dollars in
medical bills but you work hard for thirty-five
years and you pay it back and then – one day – you
have a massive stroke, your whole right side is
paralyzed, you have to limp along the streets and
speak out of the left side of your mouth and drool,
but you go into rehabilitation and regain the power
to walk and the power to talk and then – one day –
you step off a curb at Sixty-seventh Street, and
BANG! you get hit by a city bus and then you die.
Maybe.
– *DENIS LEARY*

There's only one thing more painful than
learning from experience, and that is not
learning from experience.
– *ANONYMOUS*

The thing that impresses me the most about
America is the way parents obey their children.
– *KING EDWARD VIII*

The younger members of our society are not
different from what they have always been …
At the time of the world when there were only
two young people, Cain and Abel, one of them
was a delinquent.
– *LORD ABERDARE*

There is always a moment in childhood when the
door opens and lets the future in.
– *GRAHAM GREENE*

A man must have grown old and lived long in
order to see how short life is.
– *Arthur Schopenhauer*

When a middle-aged man says in a moment
of weariness that he is half dead, he is telling
the literal truth.
– *Elmer Davis*

My salad days,
When I was green in judgment.
– *William Shakespeare*

Do you think my mind is maturing late,
Or simply rotted early?
— *OGDEN NASH*

Young men think old men are fools;
but old men know young men are fools.
— *GEORGE CHAPMAN*

Experience is the name everyone gives
to their mistakes.
— *OSCAR WILDE*

Nature makes boys and girls lovely to look upon so
they can be tolerated until they acquire some sense.
— *WILLIAM LYON PHELPS*

Being young is not having any money; being young
is not minding not having any money.
— *KATHARINE WHITEHORN*

Children have neither past nor future; they enjoy
the present, which very few of us do.
– *Jean de La Bruyère*

Experience is not what happens to a man. It is what
a man does with what happens to him.
– *Aldous Leonard Huxley*

They shall grow not old,
as we that are left grow old:
Age shall not weary them
nor the years condemn.
– *Laurence Binyon*

The tragedy of old age is not that one is old,
but that one is young.
– OSCAR WILDE

I wish I didn't know now what I didn't know then.
– BOB SEGER

Wisdom doesn't necessarily come with age.
Sometimes age just shows up all by itself.
– TOM WILSON

Youth is something very new: twenty years ago no
one mentioned it.
– GABRIELLE 'COCO' CHANEL (in 1971)

Youth is the gift of nature, but age is a work of art.
— *Stanislaw J. Lec*

I should have no objection to a
repetition of the same life from its
beginning, only asking the advantages
authors have in a second edition
to correct some faults of the first.
— *Benjamin Franklin*

Adults are obsolete children.
— *Dr Seuss*

Youth is a period of missed opportunities.
— *Cyril Connolly*

It's one of nature's ways that we often feel closer to
distant generations than to the generation
immediately preceding us.
— *Igor Stravinsky*

Growing old is mandatory; growing up is optional.
– *CHILI DAVIS*

You're only as old as the woman you feel.
– *GROUCHO MARX*

As you get older three things happen.
The first is your memory goes,
and I can't remember the other two.
– *NORMAN WISDOM*

Forty years on, growing older and older,
Shorter in wind, as in memory long,
Feeble of foot, and rheumatic of shoulder,
What will it help you that once you were strong?
– *EDWARD ERNEST BOWEN*

Once a child, always a child.
– *ANONYMOUS*

The freethinking of one age is the common
sense of the next.
– *MATTHEW ARNOLD*

I don't believe one grows older. I think that what
happens early on in life is that at a certain age one
stands still and stagnates.
– *T.S. ELIOT*

I learned … that one can never go back, that one
should not ever try to go back – that the essence
of life is going forward. Life is really a One
Way Street.
– *AGATHA CHRISTIE*

You are only young once, but you can stay
immature indefinitely.
– *ANONYMOUS*

For age is opportunity no less
Than youth itself, though in another dress,
And as the evening twilight fades away
The sky is filled with stars, invisible by day.
– *HENRY WADSWORTH LONGFELLOW*

The great secret that all old people
share is that you really haven't changed
in seventy or eighty years. Your body changes,
but you don't change at all.
And that, of course, causes great confusion.
— DORIS LESSING

The trouble with our times is that the future is
not what it used to be.
— PAUL VALERY

Age is not a particularly interesting subject. Anyone
can get old. All you have to do is live long enough.
— GROUCHO MARX

You know you're getting old when you stoop to tie
your shoelaces and wonder what else you could do
while you're down there.
— GEORGE BURNS

I tend to live in the past because most of
my life is there.
— HERB CAEN

He who controls the past controls the future: he who controls the present controls the past.
– GEORGE ORWELL

Age affects how people experience time … the years go faster as one gets older. At the age of four or six, a year seems interminable; at sixty, the years begin to blend and are frequently hard to separate from each other because they move so fast!
– EDWARD T. HALL

Age mellows some people; others it makes rotten.
— *ANONYMOUS*

Good people are good because they've come to
wisdom through failure.
— *WILLIAM SAROYAN*

It is no wonder that people are so horrible when
they start life as children.
— *KINGSLEY AMIS*

People say that age is just a state of mind. I say it's
more about the state of your body.
— *GEOFFREY PARFITT*

People who say you're just as
old as you feel are
all wrong, fortunately.
— *RUSSELL BAKER*

Adolescence is perhaps nature's way of preparing
parents to welcome the empty nest.
— *KAREN SAVAGE AND PATRICIA ADAMS*

Middle age is the awkward period when Father
Time starts catching up with Mother Nature.
— *HAROLD COFFIN*

Adolescence is a period of rapid changes. Between
the ages of twelve and seventeen, for example, a
parent ages as much as twenty years.
— *ANONYMOUS*

Youth is a perpetual intoxication; it is a fever
of the mind.
— *FRANÇOIS, DUC DE LA ROCHEFOUCAULD*

The most prolific period of pessimism comes at
twenty-one, or thereabouts, when the first attempt
is made to translate dreams into reality.
– *HEYWOOD BROUN*

What most persons consider as virtue, after the
age of forty, is simply a loss of energy.
– *VOLTAIRE*

As you get older, the pickings get slimmer, but the people don't.
— CARRIE FISHER

Anyone who uses the phrase 'easy as taking candy from a baby' has never tried taking candy from a baby.
– ANONYMOUS

If you want to stay young-looking, pick your parents very carefully.
– DICK CLARK

Old age is like a plane flying through a storm.
Once you're aboard, there's nothing you can do.
– Golda Meir

Men do not quit playing because they grow old:
they grow old because they quit playing.
– Oliver Wendell Holmes

Life is like playing a violin solo in public and
learning the instrument as one goes along.
– Samuel Butler

**There is no pleasure worth
forgoing just for an extra
three years in the geriatric ward.**
– John Mortimer

Praise youth and it will prosper.
– Irish proverb

A preoccupation with the future not only prevents us from seeing the present as it is but often prompts us to rearrange the past.
– *Eric Hoffer*

The young are preoccupied with approaching old age, while the old are preoccupied with lost youth.
– *Michael Patrick*

We are born princes and the
civilizing process makes us frogs.
— *ERIC BERNE*

The problem with beauty is that it's like being born
rich and getting poorer.
— *JOAN COLLINS*

My adolescence progressed normally:
enough misery to keep the death wish my usual
state, an occasional high to keep me from actually
taking the gas pipe.
– *FAYE MOSKOWITZ*

Of all the self-fulfilling prophecies in our culture,
the assumption that ageing means decline and poor
health is probably the deadliest.
– *MARILYN FERGUSON*

Children are a poor man's riches.
– *PROVERB*

I am in the prime of senility.
– *JOEL CHANDLER HARRIS (attributed)*

Age does not protect you from love. But love, to
some extent, protects you from age.
– *JEANNE MOREAU*

To be or not to be isn't
the question.
The question is how
to prolong being.
– *TOM ROBBINS*

Raising kids is part joy and part guerrilla warfare.
– *ED ASNER*

You know you've reached middle age when a
doctor, not a policeman, tells you to slow down,
all you exercise are your prerogatives and it takes
you longer to rest than to get tired.
– *ANONYMOUS*

We don't receive wisdom: we must discover it for ourselves after a journey that no one can take us or spare us.
— *MARCEL PROUST*

Someone once remarked that in adolescence pornography is a substitute for sex, whereas in adulthood sex is a substitute for pornography.
— *EDMUND WHITE*

It is a mistake to regard age as a downhill grade toward dissolution. The reverse is true. As one grows older, one climbs with surprising strides.
— *GEORGE SAND*

Remember that as a teenager you are in the last stage of your life when you will be happy to hear that the phone is for you.
– *FRAN LEIBOWITZ*

Age demands respect; youth, love.
– *MARY WOLLSTONECRAFT*

Nothing is more responsible for the good old days than a bad memory.
– *FRANKLIN P. ADAMS*

Retirement at sixty-five is ridiculous. When I was sixty-five I still had pimples.
– *GEORGE BURNS*

Every generation revolts against its fathers and makes friends with its grandfathers.
– *LEWIS MUMFORD*

It's sad to grow old but nice to ripen.
— *BRIGITTE BARDOT*

We thought we were running away from the
grown-ups, and now we're the grown-ups.
— *MARGARET ATWOOD*

Don't rush, eternity will wait.
— *ELLIOTT PRIEST*

Heredity is what sets the parents of a teenager
wondering about each other.
– *Laurence J. Peter*

Setting a good example for children takes all the
fun out of middle age.
– *William Feather*

Inside every seventy-year-old is a thirty-five-year-
old asking, 'What happened?'
– *Ann Landers*

The childhood shows the man
As morning shows the day.
– *JOHN MILTON*

Old people should not eat
health foods. They need all the
preservatives they can get.
– *ROBERT ORBEN*

Never lose sight of the fact that old age needs so little but needs that little so much.
– MARGARET WILLOUR

I was eleven, then I was sixteen. Though no honours came my way, those were the lovely years.
– TRUMAN CAPOTE

Old age lives minutes slowly, hours quickly; childhood chews hours and swallows minutes.
– MALCOLM DE CHAZAL

The older I get, the smarter my parents are.
– K. PRIESKORN

It is sobering to consider that when Mozart was my age he had already been dead for a year.
– TOM LEHRER

Why should society feel responsible only for the education of children, and not for the education of all adults of every age?
– ERICH FROMM

Though it sounds absurd, it is true to say I felt younger at sixty than I felt at twenty.
– *ELLEN GLASGOW*

There is always some specific moment when we become aware that our youth is gone; but, years after, we know it was much later.
– *MIGNON MCLAUGHLIN*

When it comes to staying young, a mind lift beats a face lift any day.
– *MARTY BUCELLA*

The secret of staying young is to live honestly, eat slowly and lie about your age.
– *LUCILLE BALL*

I've always thought that the stereotype of the dirty old man is really the creation of a dirty young man who wants the field to himself.
– *HUGH DOWNS*

The average teenager still has all the faults his parents outgrew.
– *ANONYMOUS*

There are children playing in the streets who could solve some of my top problems in physics, because they have modes of sensory perception that I lost long ago.
– *J. ROBERT OPPENHEIMER*

The older you get the stronger the wind gets – and it's always in your face.
– *JACK NICKLAUS*

There are three things which the superior man guards against. In youth … lust. When he is strong … quarrelsomeness. When he is old … covetousness.
– *CONFUCIUS*

Sure, I'm for helping the elderly. I'm going to be old myself some day.
– *LILLIAN CARTER (in her eighties)*

You don't have to suffer to be a poet.
Adolescence is enough suffering for anyone.
– JOHN CIARDI

I take my children everywhere, but they always
find their way back home.
– ROBERT ORBEN

O, what a tangled web do parents weave
When they think that their children are naïve.
– OGDEN NASH

Parents often talk about the
younger generation as if they didn't have
anything to do with it.
– HAIM GINOTT

We must not take the faults of our youth into our old age, for old age brings with it its own defects.
– *JOHANN WOLFGANG VON GOETHE*

The years teach much which the days never knew.
– *RALPH WALDO EMERSON*

The invention of the teenager was a mistake. Once you identify a period of life in which people get to stay out late but don't have to pay taxes – naturally, nobody wants to live any other way.
– *JUDITH MARTIN*

I am old enough to tell the truth.
It is one of the privileges of age.
— *GEORGES CLEMENCEAU*

I do wish I could tell you
my age but it's impossible.
It keeps changing all the time.
— *GREER GARSON*

There's nothing that keeps its youth,
So far as I know, but a tree and truth.
— *OLIVER WENDELL HOLMES*

Childhood is that wonderful time of life when all
you need to do to lose weight is take a bath.
— *RICHARD ZERA*

There is always a lot to be thankful for, if you take
the time to look. For example, I'm sitting here
thinking how nice it is that wrinkles don't hurt.
— *ANONYMOUS*

That which seems the height of absurdity in
one generation often becomes the height of
wisdom in another.
– ADLAI STEVENSON

A hair in the head is worth two in the brush.
– OLIVER HERFORD

And in the end it's not the years in your life that
count. It's the life in your years.
– ABRAHAM LINCOLN

The deepest definition of youth is life as yet
untouched by tragedy.
– ALFRED NORTH WHITEHEAD

**The first half of our lives is ruined by our
parents and the second half by our children.**
– CLARENCE DARROW

I am getting old and the sign of old age is that I
begin to philosophize and ponder over problems
which should not be my concern at all.
– JAWAHARLAL NEHRU

Of middle age the best that can be said is that a
middle-aged person has likely learned how to have
a little fun in spite of his troubles.
– DON MARQUIS

The older I grow the more earnestly I feel that
the few joys of childhood are the best
that life has to give.
– ELLEN GLASGOW

The tragedy of life is not that it ends so soon, but
that we wait so long to begin it.
– *ANONYMOUS*

Blessed are the young for they shall inherit
the national debt.
– *HERBERT HOOVER*

In delay there lies no plenty:
Then come kiss me, sweet and twenty,
Youth's a stuff will not endure.
– *WILLIAM SHAKESPEARE*

There are so many ways of dying, it is astonishing
that any of us choose old age.
– *BERYL BAINBRIDGE*

There is only one cure for grey hair. It was invented
by a Frenchman. It is called the guillotine.
– *P.G. WODEHOUSE*

There was no respect for youth when I was young, and now that I am old, there is no respect for age – I missed it coming and going.
— *J.B. P* RIESTLEY

About the only thing that comes to us without effort is old age.
— *G*LORIA *P*ITZER

Things do not change, we change.
— *H*ENRY *D*AVID *T*HOREAU

I do not think much of a man who is not wiser
today than he was yesterday.
– *ABRAHAM LINCOLN*

Once a man's thirty, he's already old,
He is indeed as good as dead.
'Twere best to kill him right away.
– *JOHANN WOLFGANG VON GOETHE*

After thirty, a body has a mind of its own.
– *BETTE MIDLER*

Is life worth living?
This is a question for an embryo, not for a man.
– *SAMUEL BUTLER*

The time to begin most things is ten years ago.
– *MIGNON MCLAUGHLIN*

None are so old as those who have
outlived enthusiasm.
– *HENRY DAVID THOREAU*

Those who love deeply never grow old; they may die of old age, but they die young.
– *Dorothy Canfield Fisher*

Always be nice to those younger than you, because they are the ones who will be writing about you.
– *Cyril Connolly*

Thou shouldst not have been old till thou hadst been wise.
– *William Shakespeare*

Though no one can go back and make a brand-new start, anyone can start from now and make a brand-new ending.
– *Carl Bard*

There are three ages of man – youth, age and 'you're looking wonderful'.
– *Francis Spellman*

> There's nothing wrong with the younger generation that becoming taxpayers won't cure.
> – DAN BENNETT

Experience is a great advantage. The problem is that, when you get it, you're too damned old to do anything about it.
– JIMMY CONNORS

The illusion that times that were are better than those that are has probably pervaded all ages.
– HORACE GREELEY

They talk about the economy this year. Hey, my hairline is in recession, my waistline is in inflation. Altogether, I'm in a depression.
– RICK MAJERUS

You couldn't get hold of the things you'd done
and turn them right again. Such a power might be
given to the gods, but it was not given to women
and men, and that was probably a good thing.
Had it been otherwise, people would probably die
of old age still trying to rewrite their teens.
– STEPHEN KING

Young people, nowadays, imagine that money
is everything, and when they grow older they
know it.
– OSCAR WILDE

Experience makes more timid men than it
does wise ones.
– JOSH BILLINGS

Being on the tightrope is living; everything
else is waiting.
– KARL WALLENDA

By the time we hit fifty, we have learned our
hardest lessons. We have found out that only a few
things are really important. We have learned to take
life seriously, but never ourselves.
 – *Marie Dressler*

To acquire knowledge, one must study; but to
acquire wisdom, one must observe.
 – *Marilyn vos Savant*

To get back my youth I would do anything in the world, except take exercise, get up early, or be respectable.

– OSCAR WILDE

> If you want to recapture
> your youth,
> just cut off his allowance.
> – AL BERNSTEIN

The purpose of life is to fight maturity.

– DICK WERTHIMER

There are only two ways to live your life. One is as though nothing is a miracle. The other is as though everything is a miracle.

– ALBERT EINSTEIN

Youth isn't always all it's touted to be.

– LAWANA BLACKWELL

A man of forty today has nothing to worry him but falling hair, inability to button the top button, failing vision, shortness of breath, a tendency of the collar to shut off all breathing, trembling of the kidneys to whatever tune the orchestra is playing, and a general sense of giddiness when the matter of rent is brought up.
Forty is Life's Golden Age.
– ROBERT BENCHLEY

It's never too late to have a happy childhood.
– TOM ROBBINS

One should never trust a woman who tells one her real age. A woman who would tell one that, would tell one anything.
— OSCAR WILDE

Trust one who has gone through it.
— VIRGIL

Sex after ninety is like trying to shoot pool
with a rope. Even putting my cigar in its
holder is a thrill.
– *George Burns*

I will soon be six-and-twenty. Is there
anything in the future that can possibly
console us for not being always twenty-five?
– *Lord Byron*

Those whom the gods love grow young.
– *Oscar Wilde*

Americans are getting stronger. Twenty years
ago, it took two people to carry ten dollars'
worth of groceries. Today, a five-year-old can
do it.
– *Gloria Swanson*

A man is not old until regrets take the
place of dreams.
– *John Barrymore*

Life can only be understood backward,
but it must be lived forward.
– *SØREN KIERKEGAARD*

Old age is the most unexpected of all the things
that happen to a man.
– *LEON TROTSKY*

Children are unpredictable. You never know what
inconsistency they're going to catch you in next.
– *FRANKLIN P. JONES*

True terror is to wake up one morning and discover that your high school class is running the country.
— *KURT VONNEGUT*

The trouble with using experience as a guide is that the final exam often comes first and then the lesson.
— *ANONYMOUS*

When we were children, we used to think that when we were grown up we would no longer be vulnerable. But to grow up is to accept vulnerability … To be alive is to be vulnerable.
— *MADELEINE L'ENGLE*

She may very well pass for forty-three
In the dusk, with a light behind her!
— *W.S. GILBERT*

If I'd known how old I was going to be I'd have
taken better care of myself.
– *ADOLPH ZUKOR*
(on approaching his hundredth birthday)

George Washington as a boy was ignorant of the
commonest accomplishments of youth – he could
not even lie.
– *MARK TWAIN*

It's better to waste
one's youth
than to do
nothing with it at all.
– *GEORGES COURTELINE*

Nothing is a waste of time if you use the
experience wisely.
– *AUGUSTE RODIN*

At age twenty, we worry about what others think
of us. At forty, we don't care what they think of us;
at sixty, we discover they haven't been thinking
of us at all.
– ANN LANDERS

We have children because we want immortality and
this is the most reliable way of getting it.
– WOODROW WYATT

We have two lives – the one we learn with and the
life we live after that.
– BERNARD MALAMUD

Experience is what you get when you don't get
what you want.
– DAN STANFORD

Education is learning what you didn't even
know you didn't know.
– *DANIEL J. BOORSTIN*

Advice is what we ask for when we already
know the answer but wish we didn't.
– *ERICA JONG*

Think what a better world it would be if we all,
the whole world, had cookies and milk about
three o'clock every afternoon and then lay down on
our blankets for a nap.
– *BARBARA JORDAN*

Inflation is when you pay fifteen dollars for the ten-dollar haircut you used to get for five dollars when you had hair.

– SAM EWING

Middle age is the time when a man is always thinking that in a week or two he will feel as good as ever.

– DON MARQUIS

Age only matters when one is ageing. Now that I have arrived at a great age, I might just as well be twenty.

– PABLO PICASSO

Youth is when you're allowed to stay up late on New Year's Eve. Middle age is when you're forced to.

– BILL VAUGHN

At my age I do what Mark Twain did. I get my daily paper, look at the obituaries page and if I'm not there I carry on as usual.

– PATRICK MOORE

Middle age: becoming like our parents while
fighting with our children.
– *ELLIOTT PRIEST*

A child is a person who can't understand why
someone would give away a perfectly good kitten.
– *DOUG LARSON*

**Old age is not so bad when you
consider the alternatives.**
– *MAURICE CHEVALIER*

The young man who has not wept is a savage, and
the older man who will not laugh is a fool.
— *George Santayana*

Thirty-five is when you finally get your head
together and your body starts falling apart.
— *Caryn Leschen*

No wise man ever wished to be younger.
— *Jonathan Swift*

Middle age is when work is a lot less fun and
fun is a lot more work.
– *ANONYMOUS*

It is in the thirties that we want friends.
In the forties we know they won't save us any
more than love did.
– *F. SCOTT FITZGERALD*

Be wise with speed;
A fool at forty is a fool indeed.
– *EDWARD YOUNG*

**Grow old with me!
The best is yet to be.**
– *ROBERT BROWNING*

The trick is to grow up without growing old.
– *FRANK LLOYD WRIGHT*

When all the world is young, lad,
And all the trees are green;
And every goose a swan, lad,
And every lass a queen …
– CHARLES KINGSLEY

Women are not forgiven for ageing.
Robert Redford's lines of distinction are
my old-age wrinkles.
– JANE FONDA

Few women admit their age; fewer men act theirs.
– ANONYMOUS

Youth is a wonderful thing.
What a crime to waste it on children.
– *GEORGE BERNARD SHAW*
*(also often quoted as 'What a crime to waste it
on the young')*

The man who views the world at fifty
the same as he did at twenty has
wasted thirty years of his life.
– *MUHAMMAD ALI*

A child of five would understand this. Send
someone to fetch a child of five.
– *GROUCHO MARX*

Life wouldn't be worth living if I worried over the
future as well as the present.
– *W. Somerset Maugham*

Years steal
Fire from the mind as vigour from the limb;
And Life's enchanted cup but sparkles near
the brim.
– *Lord Byron*

Wisdom outweighs any wealth.
— SOPHOCLES

I've got the brain of a four-year-old.
I'll bet he was glad to be rid of it.
— GROUCHO MARX

The years between fifty and seventy
are the hardest. You are always being
asked to do things, and yet you are not
decrepit enough to turn them down.
— T.S. ELIOT

When you're eight years old nothing
is your business.
— LENNY BRUCE

It's that second time you hear your love song sung,
Makes you think perhaps, that
Love like youth is wasted upon the young.
—1960s SONG

The good die young – because they see it's no use
living if you've got to be good.
– *JOHN BARRYMORE*

There is a fountain of youth: it is your mind, your
talents, the creativity you bring to your life and the
lives of the people you love. When you learn to tap
this source, you will truly have defeated age.
– *SOPHIA LOREN*

We turn not older with years, but newer every day.
— *EMILY DICKINSON*

There is only one thing wrong with the younger generation — a lot of us don't belong to it any more.
— *BERNARD BARUCH*

You can learn many things from children. How much patience you have, for instance.
— *FRANKLIN P. JONES*

Beware of the young doctor and the old barber.
— *BENJAMIN FRANKLIN*

You're never too old to become younger.
– *MAE WEST*

It takes a long time to become young.
– *PABLO PICASSO*

Always be nice to your children because they are
the ones who will choose your rest home.
– *PHYLLIS DILLER*

Your lordship, though not clean past your youth, hath yet some smack of age in you, some relish of the saltness of time.
– *WILLIAM SHAKESPEARE*

Never raise your hand to your children; it leaves your midsection unprotected.
– *ROBERT ORBEN*

A wasted youth is better by far than a wise and productive old age.
– *MEAT LOAF*

Crabbed age and youth cannot live together;
Youth is full of pleasance, age is full of care.
— WILLIAM SHAKESPEARE

Don't laugh at a youth for his affectations;
he is only trying on one face after another to find
a face of his own.
— LOGAN PEARSALL SMITH

If youth is the season of hope, it is often so only in
the sense that our elders are hopeful about us.
— GEORGE ELIOT

**In youth we learn;
in age we understand.**
— MARIE EBNER-ESCHENBACH

Youth is a blunder; manhood a struggle;
old age a regret.
— BENJAMIN DISRAELI

The pride of youth is in strength and beauty, the
pride of old age is in discretion.

– DEMOCRITUS

To get back one's youth one has merely
to repeat one's follies.

– OSCAR WILDE

We are only young once.
That is all society can stand.

– BOB BOWEN

SARAH JANE: Doctor, you're being childish.
THE DOCTOR: Well, of course I am. There's no point
in growing up if you can't be childish sometimes.
— *DOCTOR WHO*

You know you're getting old when the candles
cost more than the cake.
— *BOB HOPE*

> You know you're old when
> you notice how young
> the derelicts are getting.
> — JEANNE PHILLIPS

How sharper than a serpent's tooth it is
To have a thankless child!
– *WILLIAM SHAKESPEARE*

Don't bother discussing sex with small children.
They rarely have anything to add.
– *FRAN LEIBOWITZ*

I would there were no age between sixteen and
three-and-twenty, or that youth would sleep out the
rest, for there is nothing in the between but getting
wenches with child, wronging the ancientry,
stealing, fighting.
– *WILLIAM SHAKESPEARE*

Youth, large, lusty, loving —
Youth full of grace, force, fascination,
Do you know that Old Age
may come after you with
equal grace, force, fascination?
— WALT WHITMAN

Small children disturb your sleep,
big children your life.
— *YIDDISH PROVERB*

As is the mother, so is her daughter.
— *PROVERB*

To be seventy years young is sometimes far more
cheerful and hopeful than to be forty years old.
— *OLIVER WENDELL HOLMES*

We get too soon old and too late smart.
— *DUTCH PROVERB*

A happy childhood has spoiled many
a promising life.
– ROBERTSON DAVIES

In the spring a young man's fancy lightly turns
to thoughts of love.
– ALFRED, LORD TENNYSON

When children stand quiet they have done some ill.
– PROVERB

Education is what survives when what has been
learned has been forgotten.
– B.F. SKINNER

I swear she's no
chicken; she's on
the wrong side
of thirty, if she be
a day.
– JONATHAN SWIFT

An educational system isn't worth a great deal if it teaches young people how to make a living but doesn't teach them how to make a life.

– *ANONYMOUS*

He is a teenager, after all – a strange agent with holes in his jeans, studs in his ear, a tail down his neck, a cap on his head (backward).

– *ELLEN KARSH*

Telling a teenager the facts
of life is like giving
a fish a bath.
– *ARNOLD H. GLASOW*

Imagination is more important than knowledge, for knowledge is limited while imagination embraces the entire world.

– *ALBERT EINSTEIN*

Every human being on this earth is born with a tragedy, and it isn't original sin. He's born with the tragedy that he has to grow up. That he has to leave the nest, the security, and go out to do battle. He has to lose everything that is lovely and fight for a new loveliness of his own making, and it's a tragedy. A lot of people don't have the courage to do it.

– *HELEN HAYES*

Children are one third of our population and all of our future.
– *Select Panel for the Promotion of Child Health (1981)*

I don't think of the past. The only thing that matters is the everlasting present.
– *W. Somerset Maugham*

Every mother thinks her own gosling a swan.
– *Proverb*

You start out happy that you have no hips or boobs.
All of a sudden you get them, and it feels sloppy.
Then, just when you start liking them, they start
drooping.
– CINDY CRAWFORD

Middle age: when the past
was perfect,
and the present is tense.
– ELLIOTT PRIEST

Old age is no such uncomfortable thing if one gives oneself up to it with a good grace, and don't drag it about 'to midnight dances and the public show'.

– *HORACE WALPOLE, 4TH EARL OF ORFORD*

You, too, will get old.

– *KURT VONNEGUT*

Adolescence is just one big walking pimple.

– *CAROL BURNETT*

> He wears the rose
> Of youth upon him.
> — WILLIAM SHAKESPEARE

In order to know whether a human being
is young or old, offer it food of different
kinds at short intervals.
If young, it will eat anything at
any hour of the day or night.
— OLIVER WENDELL HOLMES

If you want to see what children can do,
you must stop giving them things.
– NORMAN DOUGLAS

We are all either fools or undiscovered geniuses.
– BONNIE LIN

The wisest mind has something yet to learn.
– GEORGE SANTAYANA

With the birth of each child, you lose two novels.
— *CANDIA McWILLIAM*

Experience is what you got by not having it
when you need it.
— *ANONYMOUS*

Middle age: The time when you'll do anything to
feel better, except give up what is hurting you.
— *ROBERT QUILLEN*

I think older women with younger men
threaten all the right people.
— *WILLIAM HAMILTON*

**Knowledge comes,
but wisdom lingers.**
— *ALFRED, LORD TENNYSON*

My mother loved children – she would have
given anything if I had been one.
– *GROUCHO MARX*

I'll be eighty this month. Age, if nothing else,
entitles me to set the record straight before I
dissolve. I've given my memoirs far more thought
than any of my marriages. You can't divorce a book.
– *GLORIA SWANSON*

**And youth is cruel, and has no remorse
And smiles at situations which it cannot see.
I smile of course,
And go on drinking tea.**
–T.S.ELIOT